Evidence
of
DRAGONS

Pie Corbett has advised the National Literacy Strategy for both the Primary and Key Stage 3 phase. He works across the country running inset and development projects, and was co-leader of the DfES Innovations project on 'Storymaking', based at the International Learning and Research Centre. Author of over 250 books, he writes poetry, stories and materials for teachers. He has compiled many bestselling anthologies for Macmillan Children's Books, including *The Works 2*, *The Works 4* and *Assembly Poems*. This is h

Also by Pie Corbett

The Works 4
(with Gaby Morgan)

The Works 6

The Works Key Stage 1

The Works Key Stage 2

MACMILLAN
POETRY

Evidence
of
DRAGONS

Poems by Pie Corbett

Illustrated by Peter Bailey

MACMILLAN CHILDREN'S BOOKS

To Melanie

First published 2011 by Macmillan Children's Books
a division of Macmillan Publishers Limited
20 New Wharf Road, London N1 9RR
Basingstoke and Oxford
Associated companies throughout the world
www.panmacmillan.com

ISBN 978-0-230-75194-1

1 3 5 7 9 8 6 4 2

A CIP catalogue record for this book is available from
the British Library.

Printed and bound in the UK by CPI Mackays, Chatham ME5 8TD

Contents

Praise Poem

Let us begin
   with the hottest of days
      and the shock of icy water sipped from
                         frosted glass.

Let us begin
   with the tickle of a ladybird
      and the rosebud of its freckled red coat.

Let us begin
   with the fizz of sherbet lemon
      sizzling on the tongue.

Let us begin
   with the sudden grin and giggle
      of a joke cracked open like a walnut.

Let us begin
   with the cat's warm purr
      and the first crazy petals of snow falling.

Let us begin
   with the kicking of legs
      as the swing flings itself higher.

Let us begin
    with a blade of grass
        and sunlight pouring through clouds
                            like golden dust.

Let us begin
    with the hot breath of chips on a cold night
        and the surprise of torchlight icing
                            the dark.

Let us begin
    by counting the rings on your fingertips
        and the mystery of a magnet's pull.

Yes, let us begin
with such simple things.

A Poem to Be Spoken Silently . . .

It was so silent that I heard
my thoughts rustle
like leaves in a paper bag . . .

It was so peaceful that I heard
the trees ease off
their coats of bark . . .

It was so still that I heard
the paving stones groan
as they muscled for space . . .

It was so silent that I heard
a page of this book
whisper to its neighbour,
'Look, he's peering at us again . . .'

It was so still that I felt
a raindrop grin
as it tickled the window's pane . . .

It was so calm that I sensed
a smile crack
the wary face
of a stranger . . .

It was so quiet that I heard
the morning earth roll over
in its sleep and doze
for five minutes more ...

Wings

If I had wings
    I would touch the fingertips of clouds
        and glide on the wind's breath.

If I had wings
    I would taste a chunk of the sun,
        as hot as peppered curry.

If I had wings
    I would listen to the clouds of sheep bleat
        that graze on the blue.

If I had wings
    I would breathe deep and sniff
        the scent of raindrops.

If I had wings
    I would gaze at people
        who cling to the earth.

If I had wings
    I would dream of
        swimming the deserts
            and walking the seas.

The Cloud Appreciation Society

Clouds are no bother;
they do not interfere
with anyone –
are not known to be
busybodies,
keep their noses clean.
They loiter quietly,
then shuffle on.

Clouds are cheap;
make ideal pets.
Needing no feeding,
they thrive
with no real attention.
The main advantage
of a cloud
is that it takes
no looking after.
Clouds just get on
with the job
of shepherding themselves.
You do not need a dog
to round them up.

The sun warms
a cloud's back –
the wind sculpts
its shifting form.

Dawn brings
another bunch of cloud surprises –
all shapes and sizes blossoming,
whether you like it or not.
For the work of a cloud
is never finished –
the job never done.

Perhaps it's not much fun
being a cloud . . .
but at least they have no need
to be perfect.

Nameless, they shift storms.
Blameless, they ferment lightning.

No one has ever tamed a cloud.

I like the way clouds
look after themselves
without any fuss.
A bus needs a driver,
a ship needs a sail,
but a cloud moves on
like a gigantic soft whale
slowly easing through
a sea of blue.

New clouds pillow,
billowing and blowing.
No cloud is ever the same.
You'll never find
identical clouds.

Drift on white
    mystery.
Ghost-silent,
each moment
    making
cloud
    history.

Are You Sleepwalking?

Cats are more than alive.
That purposeful purr,
the ripple
of muscle and fur;
and bright eyes seen green
in midnight
headlights . . .

But what about trees?
They too grow slow,
stretching up;
their thin limbs
covered in rough skin.
They live and die.

But is water alive?
Like us it sleeps,
still and deep –
then shifts restlessly
like wind-blown silk,
or silver pouring from a tap.
If you touch water,
it moves aside,
its wet invitation
lets you slide in.

And rocks –
may be hard as nails,
but they wear a thin skin –
a cold crust of lichen;
icy in winter,
warmed by simple sun.
Like solid old men,
weathered till
they too crumble into dust.

You must look close enough,
to enter their world –
even the grass seems alive –
as it uncurls its slim, green skin
and twists with the wind.

And what of you?
Have you yet woken to the world,
sensing its every move?
Or are you sleepwalking
through every waking moment?

Watching

Watching
   the red admiral's miracle,
      the opening and closing of wings,
      the gentle fluttering of prayer flags

and the peacocks clustering
   on the purple buddleia.

Watching their dusty colours
   and silks flickering.

Watching the tubby bees
   noisily nudging for a space,
   nectar-greedy.

Watching
   the sunlight catching
      the flowers and speared leaves,
      describing shadows,

and I'm thinking
   how many of the small things
   that I love are free for those

who know
> how to see for themselves
> > the miraculous and commonplace
> > so close to hand –

the ant's hieroglyphic trail;
> the snail's slow determination;
> > even the money spider –
> > > that pinprick of blood,
> > > > perfect on a red-brick wall.

Go into –

a river as it noses by
burrowing between banks,
carving through stone.

Within it must be lonely;
except for the constant chatter
of stones rattling along;
except for the slither
of eels and the silver of fish.

Go in –
you might find the sky
or the moon or your own face
staring back.

Inside, there is the rush
of waterfalls and a wave's curve;
the imprint of a whale
and the dark shadow of a shark.

Go in –
it will wash away
the day's dirt and some may be
dazzled by its power
to free the soul
from sin – so, dip in –
it may not be as cold
as you fear.

Spain – Summer Diary 2001

Cicadas buzz
like electricity.

It's so hot that
wasps and bees drink
from the swimming pool.

Ants carry off trophies from our meal.

Stunned by sun.
Heat bounces
off whitewashed walls.
The track ahead shimmers.

Flies irritate –
whining,
stalking the cup's rim –
settling on my hand.

Towels map the washing line –
the breeze quivers –
a distant lorry tugs uphill.

Cicadas are busy.
The hillside seems alive.

14

Inside the fridge hums.
The landscape does nothing too.

Clouds   drift   my thoughts

    distant hills –
like a sleeping lion –
    crouch.

    The sun steadily
        turns up the temperature.

Pastel-blue dragonflies,
    pencil-slim,
        hover by the pool.

Daisy's wasp sting –
    a white injection mark –
        like a tiny, raised moon.

        It's three o'clock at night.
        Lightning bursts over mountains
    in a purple fuzz.

Trying to sleep but
    the room is too stuffy –
    even the pillows sweat.

Moon crumbles   night swim   stars scatter

The Things Around You

Make use of the things around you,
suggested Raymond Carver –
the man sitting opposite me
on the 5.15 to Leicester sips sweet tea.
His styrofoam cup sweats.
The Twix bar glitters false bronze.
Water bubbles in my lemonade rise and pop.
The tap of computers by commuters
punctuates the train's rumble.
The low hum of conversation
and awkward glances pass the time.
A mum leans forwards to swap gossip with her
    daughter;
both dressed in tank tops and jeans
they address their faces; stroking their darkening
    eyebrows.
Reflections ghost the train window;
my mirror image gazes back.
Beyond, the black river slides by.
Towns glide past like dark swans.
Road lights are bright-orange necklaces.
A motorway becomes an artery.

Wellingborough station is a cold shadow.
Passengers pace, restless with waiting.
The display board marks time and I'm
making the most of the 5.15 to Leicester,
carving up the things around me.

City Jungle

Rain splinters town.
   Lizard cars cruise by;
their radiators grin.

Thin headlights stare –
   shop doorways keep
their mouths shut.

At the roadside
   hunched houses cough.

Newspapers shuffle by,
   hands in their pockets.
The gutter gargles.

A motorbike snarls;
   dustbins flinch.

Street lights bare
   their yellow teeth.
The motorway's
   cat-black tongue
lashes across
   the glistening back
of the tarmac night.

Biking Free

Black tyres spin –
patterns tread –
spokes flicker –
legs of lead.

Steel rim squeals –
brake blocks clasp –
squeeze as hard –
as a bully's grasp.

Streets blur by –
eyeball stings –
handles gleam –
cycle sings.

Pounding pulse –
heartbeats race –
clicking gears –
furious pace.

The Gathering

November clouds bunch
together –

hunching their cold, grey shoulders
against the day's sharp wind.

Thin trees drift
their spindly limbs;

ivy on the drystone wall
lifts and falls with each shuddering breath.

A crow falters mid-flight,
dips its bright-black wing-tips;

a ragged flag that slips
through the wind's invisible tide.

Rain slings itself against the windowpane
while the night gathers boulders of darkness,

stacks up racks of cloud.
The moon is a castaway on an island of stone.

Lone stars are lost sheep.
Sleep greedily gathers the silence.

Winter Haiku –
23 December 2003

Bitter dawn wind bites
  like a dog – clouds are sly cats
    slipping quietly by.

      Frozen puddles – leaves
        locked in ice, suspended in
          a slice of cold time.

        Frosted grass catches
          sunlight – it glitters like
            glass-splintered forests.

          Snow drifts across town
            in a swarm; a soft, white storm
              kidnapping the streets.

        This morning the moon
          is a ghostly thumbprint traced
            on shivers of blue.

      Winter dawn – the milk
        bottles are frosted; cars skid,
      cat-screech down the street.

Early Winter Diary Poem

Six thirty;
   winter dawn –

scraping a thin skin
   of frost
from the windscreen –
   numb fingers fumble –
even the spray freezes.
   The breeze is bitter –
it's so cold
   that stones crack –
that wool freezes
   on the sheep's back.

The birds are too still –
   even the sun
turns its back
   on the day;
but lazy woodsmoke
   idles
over Minchin's roof.

(18 November 1999)

Narnia Changing Seasons

1. Winter, Always Winter

In winter –
Snow sculpts the trees.
Icicles hang like goblins' teeth.
Ponds are polished mirrors.
Puddles are shiny shields of glass.
Ice crackles underfoot.
Brittle leaves drift like a pack of cold cards
spilt from Jack Frost's hand.
White blades of grass jut up.
Frail frost glitters on the mountain paths,
snowflakes swarm,
moulding the fields,
powdering the hedges,
dusting the lanes in icing sugar,
transforming trees, softening edges,
settling quietly on window ledges,
blinding fields in a bandage of white.
Sparrows sit hunched in fir trees,
fluffing feathers to keep warm.
Leaves are crisp and cold.
Beneath the frozen roots of trees,
the woodland creatures huddle.
Snow crunches.
Puddles splinter.

Between the fir trees
a lamp post glows,
throws a pool of warm light
on white snow –
and in the distant darkness
the White Queen's palace waits
behind black metal gates
for the sons and daughters
of Adam and Eve
who will grieve their loss
to the dumb heart of winter.

2. Spring Awakes

When spring breaks –
snow melts,
icicles drip from trees,
streams flow with mountain snow,
green spring blades fist through soft earth.
Primroses burst on to mossy banks
like a thousand soft stars.
Crocuses burst open
in a scatter of purple and yellow,
daffodils blow their trumpets.
Buds burst on branches,
while leaves uncurl
and shake themselves awake
into the warm breeze.

Rabbits sneeze and snuffle.
Clouds loiter like old man's beard
drifting by – the sky is sheer blue.
Sparrows chatter in hedgerows.
Squirrels natter in treetops.
Bees busy themselves.
Lambs on hillsides like white jumpers.
The rooks cackle in tall trees,
their ragged nests like spidery caps.
At night, old badger stirs from his long sleep,
creeps outside, yawns and sniffs spring air.
And out of the darkness
the nightingale sings –
springing the cold world awake.

Dawn breaks.
Morning shakes its sleepy head
and the forest shimmers.
Sunlight glimmers on spidery webs.
Butterflies stumble, tumbling
like tiny coloured flags.
The great stags flex their antlers.

In the warmth
the White Queen shivers
as the rivers sing and the spring earth rings.

Walking Backwards

The wind blew
so hard down Farm Lane
that we had to walk
backwards –
buffeted
by icy blasts.

Holding our coats skintight,
blundering backwards,
into the icy night,
laughing aloud,
our voices lost
on the wind's teeth.

Not able to see
where we were going,
we staggered forwards,
stumbling backwards
from Poppy's house
into the New Year.

(31 December 2004)

Sunday Morning Diary Poem

This Sunday morning
surprised by birdsong.
Sun warms roofs,
casts cool sharp shadows –

though the road glitters.
Frost gilds
      each
         step.

Daisy and Teddy
run on ahead,
their voices echo
up the narrow lane
to Sunday school.

A marmalade cat
sneaks by greystone walls,
a blackbird sets off an alarm,
calls an early warning . . .

Trees are still skeletal,
form stark patterns
against a blue sky.

After weeks of grey fog
and sudden snow –
it feels good
to know the sun's
kindly glow –

to catch birdsong
as it drifts along
the lanes.

Early Morning, Bradford

Frost glitters
on grey pavements.

The red-bricked terrace
hunches the hillside.

A wintry wind
grips the streets,

slips down backyards

till shy sunlight
slyly catches the mosque

and its golden dome
gleams!

Joy sparks
amongst cold grey –
welcoming the day.

Poem for Poppy

Your neck of the woods was mine –
where the whale-backed hills rolled green,
where the busy spring buds burst,
where May blossom speckled the hedgerows,
where the hawk hung high,
where the skylark dizzied itself in the blue air
and violets dotted downland paths.

Where the sun shimmered on tarmac,
where the swallows dived in blue like tiny anchors,
where clouds drifted by,
where the trout flickered silver,
where the dragonfly hovered,
where the hedges smelt of thyme
and at night the moon hung like a bear's claw.

Where the winds shivered through the corn,
where the leaves fell like a deck of calling cards,
where chestnuts blossomed like tiny green bombs,
where apples blushed and raspberries fattened,
where lightning crackled an electric vein,
where lanterns lit Halloween windows
and pumpkins glowed like moons.

Where snow camouflaged the stone walls,
where the sheep's wool clung to the barbed-wire
    fence,
where puddles froze and the hills crouched,
where the stars glittered and the fields turned to
    steel.

Yes, your neck of the woods was mine
        when I was younger
and the world was so strong
        that I could taste each day.

After Reading Shelley

Let the axe strike the root,
the poison-tree will fall.

Let the rain dampen the dirt,
the dust will start to bud.

Let the sun break the night,
the dark will disappear.

Let the dam hold the flow,
the river will not flood.

Let the ship carve the course,
the waves will fall aside.

Let the wind move the trees,
the branch will turn its head.

Let the spade slice the earth,
the soil will open wide.

Let the hand stop the fist,
the anger may embrace.

Let the song start to dance,
the soul will lift its face.

After Reading Carl Sandburg

The night is
sensitive in the slip of a shadow,
sliding on a dress of darkness.

The wind is
playing Chinese whispers
till its message
is lost in the trees.

The rain is
tapping at the back door,
rapping on the windowpanes,
waking up the neighbourhood.

The lightning is
like a jagged scar
across the dark belly
of the universe.

The thunder is
grumbling like
an old man
mumbling about
the sorry state of affairs.

The dawn is
   yawning.
      Morning opens
      its hopeful eyes.

The sun is
shouting about
in the backyard;
blistering skin
with its fiery fingers.

The Day's Eye

The sun rises,
surprises the weary night
like a sudden joke.
Daylight.

The sun gleams,
beams kindly heat
like an oven's plate.
Streets sweat.

The sun sneaks,
peeks through misty cloud
like a sly thief
alone in a crowd.

The sun sleeps,
creeps into cool shade
like a honey cat.
Shadows fade.

The sun slips,
dips into night
like a closing mouth
swallowing light.

A Brick Is Not a Beautiful Thing

A brick is not a beautiful thing.

It's not like a kingfisher
cutting a dash
in its flashy coat of blues and scarlet.

It's not like a dandelion
shaking its ruff of gold.

It's not like a Siamese cat's eyes;
that fiery stare of Egyptian sapphire.

It's not like the owl's beak
curved like a butcher's hook.

It's not like the wind
goose-pimpling your arm.

It's not like the hedgerow buds'
sudden green explosion.

No, a brick is not a beautiful thing.
It will never sing.

Sticky Beak

Our cat is a sticky beak – she

peeks
      into
            boxes –

sneaks
      under
            chairs –

dares
      to
            creep

on to
      table-
            tops –

hops
      on to
            shelves –

delves
      into
            cups –

sups
  sips
    of milk –

silky
  and
    sleek –

leaps
  at
    flies –

sleeps
  under
    the gooseberry bush –

eyes
  tight
    as fists.

Toad

Old toad sits;
squat as a fist
tightly bunched,
his legs hunched –
a grasshopper
ready to jump.

Bar-room bruiser,
baggy suited,
burly schmoozer.
Beaded eyes
blink back black.
Looks like the plague,
all mumps and bumps.

Unruffled toff.
He shuffles off,
squeezes under
a damp stone.
Then shape-shifts –
turns to granite;
fits in – sits tight.

The cat sniffs twice,
pokes with a wary paw
this crumpled intruder
who's now moved in
by the back door.

Bee

That furry busybody
bustles along hedgerows,
sticks in its nose
with inquisitive haste,
relentless in pollen-pursuit.

Golden-booted beauty;
bristling over clover,
restless where sun blazes
in a maze of scents.

The bee brings news
of new patches to cruise;
like a flying fuse
sizzling across hedgerows,
mapping fields
by whatever might yield
even the slightest flake
of gold.

Bold, sensory spy,
unaware that its one bright trick
will turn blossom
into forests.

(Stroud is about to become the first Bee Guardian Town)

My Brother's Pig

Who – grew till he was longer than a door,
    with tobacco-stained tusks like handles.

Was – big and bulky as baggage for India,
    with skin as tough as canvas.

His – hairy back as rough as a stiff brush
    and the curl of a corkscrew for a tail.

Friend – that grunted a muddy welcome
    as he munched acorns like boiled sweets.

And – he lay like a walrus alone
    in the hot dark of his shed.

Strange – that he whistled when he blew
    bubbles of spit from his nostrils.

Pet – better than a goldfish,
    for at night he crunched chunks
    from the stars.

Owl

Owl
was darker
than ebony –
flew through the night,
eyes like amber searchlights,
rested on a post,
feathers wind-ruffled,
stood stump still,
talons ready to seize
and squeeze.

Owl
was death –
that swamped the fields –
for it flew through the dark
that tightened its knot,
that bandaged the hills
in a blindfold of fear.

Owl flew – who – who – who . . .

Galilee

I remember rowing
on the lake late at night –

with the town lights dancing
on the waves –

and the sweet smell
of orange blossom drifting

from the dry banks

where we stopped to see
where Jesus walked upon the water

and the hillside where he
fed the crowd bread and fishes –

and near the border
in Rosh Pinna

we sipped tea
and stared across

at the Golan Heights –

as a hummingbird whirred
as it too sipped

from the beak of a scarlet flower –

and today as the bombs thud
I remember that dusty land,

I remember

eating a slice of sweet watermelon
like a clown's smile

from a child's painting.

Autobiography – Part One

1. Standing outside in the snow with my brothers.
   The door
slammed shut. The backlight shining.
Walking over the road to the well, dragging a
   bucket.
Three of us, sitting outside in the tin bath.
Listening to stories and songs on the radio.
Green wallpaper. The cold front room where we
   never went.
The push and shove of love; the wasp-sting of razor
   words.

2. Standing in the playground at my first school.
   Quite lost.
So many big children; not knowing what to do or
   where to
go. Like an early explorer, I felt that if I crossed the
   playground
I might not be able to find my way back across the
   grey ocean.
Assembly; sitting on the shiny wooden floor staring
   at the
cracks. Singing hymns and having to mouth the
   words aloud.
Alone in the crowd, watching clouds drift by the
   jam-jars on the classroom window. Powder
   paints. Writing till my arm

ached. The mystery of mathematics. Impossible
   tables.
Watching tadpoles spin round in the class goldfish
   globe.

3. Falling off the back of a trailer. Breaking my
   arm.
Feeling my leg snap and waiting, twisted on the
   ground.
The sharp sting of a slap.

4. Moving from the village to the farm when my
   grandfather
died. Sunlight waking me every morning.
Found one winter in the snow, my black and white
   kitten.
Walking in the woods. Damming streams. Sheep
   buried in snow.

5. Holidays. At the beach –
   waves wrinkling the sea.
Walking with no shoes on.
   The water so cold it hurt.
   My
Dad carrying me upstairs on
   his shoulders. Silent now.

Remembering

Looking at the street lights' broken reflection on
    rainy pavements.
Looking at the boarded-up shop windows, the
    empty bus-shelters and grey rain haunting the
    seafront.
Looking at frost pots blossoming beneath apple
    trees.
Looking at my budgie Charlie pecking seeds and
    chatting to his mirror.

Tasting the salt of bacon curled crisp from the grill.
Tasting the sudden tang of fizzy lemonade for the
    first surprising time.
Tasting the thick, sweet crunch of sugar crusted on
    a lardy cake.
Tasting the sand in the sandwiches and the hot bite
    of tea on a cold seaside day.

Smelling the soft mystery of my first ever peach.
Smelling the petrol in a can, hidden in the dark
    barn.
Smelling the blocked drains, the dampness of earth
    and the hot stink of the goats' shed.
Smelling bluebells and the slow silence of the little
    wood.

Touching the knotted fur on Ali the dog.
Touching the bony hand of my grandmother and
  shuddering.
Touching the icy railings on a wintry morning;
  feeling the cold stick.
Touching grass, earth, roots, tree bark, leaves, the
  sun on my face and the shimmer of insects.

Listening to the television mumbling below my
  room at night.
Listening to words sharper than a wasp sting and
  slammed doors that left me fearful.
Listening to my cat's contentment purr.
Listening to the sharp screech of brakes as a car
  halts.
Listening to stories and poems as I sat –
  comfortably.
Listening now to my own memories.

Smelling Rats

My mother said she'd 'smelt a rat',
but none of us knew what she meant.
I wondered what a rat smelt like –
they lived in sewers, Gerald said,
where they grew big as tomcats.
If cornered would go for the throat.
They made brief film appearances,
dancing on Dracula's coffin.
Gangsters muttered 'you dirty rat';
scientists kept them in cages,
testing lipstick and disease.
They ran on to boats up anchor lines
and of course we all knew
that they carried the plague.
Bubonic plague. 'BEW BON NICK . . .'
We whispered the words
so Mum wouldn't hear
and sniffed deep
but smelt nothing.

So we left her to hunt for the rat
and ran down the garden calling,
'Bring out your dead!'

Later that night I lay in bed
and heard the dread sound
of whatever it was that she sensed.
Alone in the dark, I sniffed . . .

The Warning

My mother had warned me
often enough –

but I took no notice,
thought myself tough –

as soon as her back was turned
I legged it – down town,
where I mucked about
with the free-range guys.

It was just a dare –
high up on the town wall.
So small and frail,
yet I climbed
as the town clock chimed.

Showing off,
bragging and boasting,
I sat there, legs dangling,
laughing into the face
of the wind –
and the town below
like a miniature world.

For that moment I was King –
till I felt a sudden jolt
and was hurled down,
tumbling till I took a crack,
smack on the head – like Jack;
broke my crown,
cracked my back.

'Listen,' I whispered,
'I was pushed!'

Verbal Zoo

We lioned down the corridor
elephanting and parroting
out into the sound
of the jungle playground.
The gang panthered after us
but we pigeoned by the sheds,
our heads hippoed
in a swarm of bushes.

My heart vultured –
we hedgehogged
and turtled not to monkey.

The gang of boys lioned
round the sheds –
giraffing and weasling for us.
They heroned into bushes,
beagled and eagled up trees.

After a while,
with a jackal smile,
they pythoned off
to trout about on the swings.

We butterflied wings
from our chameleon place.
My clothes were porcupined.
Mum would kangeroo me.

A Chance in France

'Stay at home,'
Mum said,

But I
took a chance
in France,
turned grey
for the day
in St Tropez,

forgot what
I did
in Madrid,
had some tussles
in Brussels
with a trio
from Rio,
lost my way
in Bombay,
nothing wrong
in Hong Kong,
felt calmer
in Palma
and quite nice
in Nice,
yes, felt finer
in China,
took a room

in Khartoum
and a villa
in Manila,
had a 'do'
in Peru
with a llama
from Lima,
took a walk
in New York
with a man
from Milan,
lost a sneaker
in Costa Rica,
got lumbago
in Tobago,
felt a menace
in Venice,
was a bore
in Singapore,
lost an ear
in Korea,
some weight
in Kuwait,
tried my best
as a guest
in old Bucharest,
got the fleas
in Belize . . .
and then
I came home.

Take Note

Elephants and
hippos are banned.
Punk rock too
might get out of hand
and there is absolutely no room
for desert islands –
they tend to be too huge and heavy,
matted with hairy trees
and slow-grown undergrowth.

Sloths are not permitted
to hang about –
trout are considered
to be slippery customers
and will not be allowed entry.

Spiders and woodlice will be
guaranteed new housing.
Curtains must keep silent
and carpets sworn to secrecy.
Yogurt will not be allowed –
while cities are considered
too much of a crowd.

Double-decker buses
would look out of place
and faces with fangs
that drip blood are barred.
Mud would be hard to contain –
and any use of the word 'mathematics'
is a calculated risk.

Brothers and sisters
are frisked before entry and
adults who throw
their mouths about
will not even be considered.

Take note –
and be warned –
this is my room.

Shadow Puppets – to My Brother Tom, in Australia

At night
we made shadow puppets.

Interlocking thumbs
and spreading fingers,
my hands became
an eagle's wings
that flew across
our bedroom wall,
caught in torchlight,
trapped in the searchlight
like a moth flame-fluttering.

Then I'd press
my first finger-pad
tight to my thumbprint
like a beak
and arch my other fingers
to make an eye.

Our hands whispered
like strange, excited birds.

That was forty years ago
and some nights now,
when the distance between us
is impossible,
I think back to when
we huddled together
and turned our hands
into shadow creatures

and once again
I let my eagle fly
across time, back to you,
warm and affectionate,
out across my bedroom wall,
out across the great oceans

and I imagine its fluid wings
etched black
on your bedroom wall,
in distant Melbourne,
10,000 miles and a world away
from the days when
we spoke with our hands
in tongues of flame.

The Homecoming – for Emaia

For a moment we burn so bright;
and then, in one cruel second,
we are gone.

While time was out
pacing the porch,
walking the dog up the back lane,
grief came calling –
left us stunned.

At first we shunned the world;
the pain swallowed us quite whole;
it took its shabby toll
upon our lives.

And waking then, we wondered, again and again,
what will become of her?
Surely she will come back –
reborn into each sweet atom
of the moth's dumb dance –
or balanced on the candle's wick,
fluid and impossibly golden.
Perhaps she will come back
as the bewildered scent of a bluebell
or the pollen brushing a bee's leg.

Perhaps she will surprise you
in an ant's sudden tickle –
or the fickle spider's sticky web.

Whatever happens –
she will come back
to be a part of all that delights
and surrounds you.

Tonight, as greedy grief eats
at your soul
and frightens you,
she is free enough already –

wandering still
where the hurt heart yearns;
where the piercing pain burns;
it seems we cannot yet shake off our grief.

Yes, life passes – too brief.
We read each other –
a library of lives
lit by sudden loving –
page upon page,
age upon age,
sweet memory laced
by sweet memory.

Graced by passing lives.
So we are lit –
and live on.

Stars

Stars

are to reach for,
beautiful freckles of hope,
speckles on velvet,
to steer ships,
to comfort those trapped
in the darkness of their making,
to lead the wayward when the compass falters,
to remind us that the day is almost breaking,
dawn is just out –
taking time to warm
the other side of the world.

Stars are for wishes.

Stars are
tiny lights of hope,
fireflies in the night,
golden specs to gaze at,
tin tacks on a dark cloth,
studs glittering,
sequins on a first party dress.

Stars are
our brightest and best,
shards of hope to keep us going,
marking the place,
making the seasons,
giving us reasons

because somewhere out there

there are other stargazers
gazing back.

The Poetman – Part One

The Poetman calls
at each house in the early hours.

When the stars are frosted flowers
and the night a velvet mole,
the Poetman shoulders his bundle.

At each doorstep he sheds a poem or two.
His whistle surprises the dark,

like a waking spell.
Dogs bark back a greeting.
Cats arch and purr.

In bedrooms children stir.
The moon grins
a thin-lipped smile.

Wily poems, like fragile reptiles,
slither indoors.
Still curled in our beds,

our dreamy heads
visit imagined shores
as the words seep though
the brain's sleeping pores.

The Poetman – Part Two

The night breathes dreams.
Only a tap drips
as I dip into
the pool of possibilities.
Stars ignore me.
The moon has failed

to show but ideas glow.
Like fireflies, words
illuminate the dark.

A whisper glistens.
Words listen for lost companions.

The imagination sends in a cat;
green-eyed, it slips
into the poem . . .
and curls up on the last line
like a question mark.
Uncertain, the dark waits outside

to be let in on cold paws;
tired, it slides through curtains,
demanding to be fed.

The poem closes its eyes.
Sleep is a disguise
for our dreams.

The Inventor's Wife Speaks

'He was up late last night
inventing planets,

Sitting at his Workmate bench,
rolling stars between finger and thumb.

Then waiting
while they fired in the furnace to a thousand
   degrees.

He left them
on the windowsill to cool beneath moonlight.

Like tiny marbles
washed sea green, cloud softened and sky blue.

Tonight he'll be up late too –
it's always the same, the second night –

creatures to create,
planets to propagate –

he'll be crouched over his microscope,
tweezers in hand, hunched like eternity's question
   mark,

worrying in the dark,
soldiering fragments from his imagination.

Why only last week
he showed me a butterfly elephant nimble as a bee –

sipping nectar through its tiny trunk,
bumbling and stumbling, an aerodynamic
    impossibility.

Then when he's finished
he'll take to his bed, sleep deep and dream

more incredible and lovely planets,
many moons, stupendous suns and new skies.'

The Secret Poem

My secret is made from –
the fingertips of candyfloss clouds,
the silent shroud between hospital heartbeats,
the hangman's cold greeting,
the stoat's winter coat
and the red-throated heron.

I found it –
trapped on the edge of a lemon's bite,
crouched tight in a crocus,
caged in a crisp packet,
crumpled at the side of the road
where the toad squats like a rock's fist.

This secret can –
prise open hearts made of steel,
smooth the surreal sea flat,
cup the cat's purr
in an empty palm,
and break apart Mount Everest
till it is powder
in a locket.

If I lost this secret –
even the lonely goat left at the roadside
would bleat . . .

A Necklace Poem by Numbers

One is the sun stuck in the sky.
Two is the pupil in a teacher's eye.

Three is the gasp after a joke.
Four is the ring made by smoke.

Five is a circle that appeared in a field.
Six is a Viking holding a shield.

Seven is found under a chair.
Eight is an eye fixing a stare.

Nine is the moon trapped in a lake.
Ten is a cake starting to bake.

Eleven is the end of the cuckoo's call.
Twelve is the beach complete with a ball.

Thirteen is the top of the circus tent.
Fourteen is the kiss that was never sent.

Fifteen is a freckle on a baby's nose.
Sixteen is the heart of a lover's rose.

Seventeen is the wheel in a hamster's cage.
Eighteen is the stop at the end of this page.

The Angel

Last night
I dreamed an angel
into our garden,

blown off course
from heaven to hell.

Dreamed he took shelter
and slept beneath the apple tree
at the end of the lawn;
his ragged wings wept,
a shroud over his shorn head.

When I woke this morning,
I looked across the garden
and knew that he was dead.

There he was,
stretched out on the lawn,
like some great swan.
His head held
beneath broken wings.

I ran out to check his pulse.
But looking into his eyes
all that I could find
were the lost skies
of some distant struggle.

Paler than chalk,
his skin too cool to touch.
I knew then
that he was dead.

So I stooped
to stroke
his fallen head
and I kissed his hair,

and as my lips
touched his cold brow,
and as my kiss
warmed his marble skin,

69

somehow his thin body shuddered
and a glow of heat shimmered
through his limbs.
Warm and alive,
he stretched his wings,
now no longer ragged,

and his golden laugh
spilt out across
our dew-drenched lawn,
filling that dawn
with a joy that bubbled
through every blade of grass,
and left the clouds lit
by its own peculiar light.

I dreamed an angel late last night
but now no one believes me.
I keep a feather of bright light
hidden beneath my bed;
just in case one of my friends
ditches disbelief;
just in case one of
    my friends
grows instead
whatever it might
    be
that to their cost
those friends have
    sadly lost.

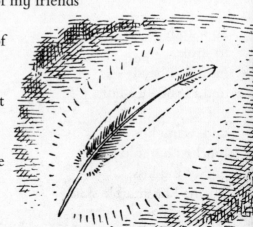

The Tale of the Giant with No Heart

A giant kept a princess
in a lonely stone tower

and every time she cried
he bought her a flower

and every time she begged him
he shook his heartless head

and every time she sobbed
she wished that she was dead.

So he took her tears
and a thimble he filled

but he dared not taste
her grief distilled.

He bought her a red rose
in a crystal flask

and he bought her a locket
but she set him a task.

'Oh if you love me truly,'
the Princess said,

'You'll find me your heart
and then we will wed.'

So, he searched in the rivers
and he searched in the trees

and he searched in the mountains
and he searched on the breeze

and all that he found
was an empty shell
with the yolk sucked dry
at the bottom of a well.

So he brought back some honey
and an old billy goat
and a bright red ribbon
to tie round her throat.

But tired with the waiting
and the years of grief
the princess's life
hung like a leaf.

It hung like a leaf
on an autumn tree
and the giant knelt down
upon one knee.

'All that I wanted
    was to dance at the ball
    with the fairest princess
    of them all.'

He unlocked the door
and climbed up the stair

and howled when he found
her, lying there . . .

He broke down the tower
and he set her free
and she smiled as she sailed
across the sea.

Farewell to the lover
she had never kissed.
Farewell to the lover
she would never miss.

And he waved
from the clifftop
and he cried
as she went

and he ached
in the heart
that True Love
had sent.

Then he sipped
from the thimble
the tears
she had shed

and he lay
in the corn
till his heart
was dead . . .

Yes, he lay
in the corn
till the sun
turned red.

The Tale of the Cleverest Son

Once, not twice,
but once, there lived
an elderly man
with sons – one, two, three.
Knowing
he would soon be dead,
he called them to his bed
and said –

'I have decided
that when I die
the cleverest of three
should receive all that I have
in this world . . .'
And on to the table he hurled
three coins.
'Take one each
and go into town.
Buy what you like.
The one
who can fill
this room with the most
will inherit all that I own.'

With a groan,
the oldest filled
a wagon with bales of straw.
The second son killed
a farmyard of turkeys;
filled sack after sack
with feathers.
But the third
slipped into a shop
and bought two
small packets
that he tucked out of sight.

That night
the father called his sons
to show how wisely
they had spent.

The oldest lad
emptied the wagon
but the straw only
covered the floor.
The second son
dragged up the sacks
and feathers flew
in all directions
but they too soon settled back,
barely covering the carpet.

Then the youngest son
took out two small packets
and a moment later
he had filled the room . . .

Now my question to you
is simply this –
what was it
that so easily flooded
the room . . . ?

Answer below

No scandal –
he bought a candle –
no catch –
he bought a match
and let light
dispel gloom
to fill the room.

The Redundant Halloween Cat

'It was after Halloween.
Well, there's not so much call
for black cats to be seen
balanced upon broomsticks.

You need a steady head
for heights and, quite frankly,
I'd got pretty fed up
with that late-night chanting.

She would serve up fried frogs
with a hot batwing stew
and the tails of dead dogs,
washed down with a brew

of toads' eyes and dried fruit.
We dined on lizard paste
and ate fish-fingered newt.
What it did to my waist

left much to be desired.
She fed me spider crisps!
I knew that she would fire
me soon enough, for I

hated her dirty jokes –
the sudden explosions
and puffs of green smoke
from bubbling cauldrons.

She kept jars of blood, dried.
I'm lucky to escape
from being "froggified".
I'm hanging up my cape.

It's time to take a break,
a spell out for a while.
Perhaps I'll undertake
to cater for a witch

with a line in fish pie
and airing-cupboard door
that could be opened up
by any agile paw.

Next year? A job with purrrks.
An in-house mouse bonus scheme.
I'll only go to work
for tax-free company cream.'

Shy Dragon

I met a shy dragon;
tucked beneath the hedgerow,
blended into the green of leaves;
the sudden darkness; the brown of bark.

Its eyes
were a betrayal –
blinking a nervous red,
with eyelids gilded gold.
It gave me a cold stare
and its snake-tongue flickered.
Claws dug deep into soil.
It sat on a clutch of
precious stones.
Its jagged tail coiled
on a nest of bleached bones.
A whisp of ragged mist marked the place.

It was early one morning
when the dew sparkled on spiders' webs –
just as the day was shaking off the rags
of night and waking itself.
Mist still slouched in the valley;
many had not yet finished dreaming,
but for me it seemed quite possible
that a miracle could occur –
if I sought hard enough.

The Dragon Whistler

The Dragon Whistler
tucks stars into her pocket,
reaches far for a sunset;
purses her moonlit lips
and whistles . . .

she listens as
owls flutter,
hedgerows mutter
and the darkness scowls –

a dragon's eye blinks
as a chink of moonlight
slinks through the cave's grime.

Again and again
the whistle bristles
in the hot silence
of the dragon's brain.

The Dragon Whistler's call
drifts across carved valleys
and mountain peaks,
seeking the dragon's lair
where rusted swords rustle,
crusted crowns tussle
and the clink of coins chimes

as the dragons fly
and the Dragon Whistler
waits, still as the moon.
For soon, they will come.

Evidence of a Dragon
(notes taken from The Dragon Tracker's Manual*)*

Large enough, most can be
identified from a safe distance.

(However, the Redhill Ridge-back
is only the size of a puppy
and therefore hides with ease.)

When seeking dragons, take care
to look for telltale signs –
trees may be stripped bare
of leaves, bark will be charred.
It should not be hard
to find scorch marks on walls
and, of course, the smouldering
remains of buildings
are a good indicator
that a dragon has passed your way.

After a dragon has called –
houses, shops and town centres
are deserted –
front doors left open,
unfinished meals on tabletops,
and TVs still blaring.

A daring dragon will rob shops,
leaving the butcher's empty.
The chewed remains of cattle are
a dead giveaway.

Dragon tracks are hard to miss –
even by the least experienced of hunters.
So too are places where trees,
bushes and sheds have been blown over.

(Remember – the force from
a full-grown dragon's wings
is as powerful as a hurricane.)

Of course, claw marks raking the earth,
turf scratched and scars on pavements
or tarmac roads all indicate a dragon's presence.

Fragments of broken shell
and piles of jewels
suggest an abandoned dragon's nest
and should be treated with caution
in case the owner returns
and burns anyone
caught loitering nearby.

Any sighting of a dragon flying,
at rest, or on the move
should be reported at once
To the DPD
(Dragon Prevention Department),
who will attempt to tempt
the dragon to kiss a princess
and fall into a hundred years
of blissful sleep.

PS
Vacancies exist
for any princess
who will not be missed!

The Last Unicorn

I am the last unicorn.
My time is starved.

I live in a cavern,
where crystals glisten
like a startled serpent's eyes.

I stare starry-eyed at the endless skies,
see frozen stars somersault.

I listen to the stark trees shiver
as the breeze slithers by.

I eat starched clouds
and old man's beard,
tugged by starlings from the hillside
where the giant of chalk stalks.

I touch the weeping rain
and breathe the fine wine of starlight.

I sniff the scent of skeleton leaves
abandoned by autumn
like frozen starfish.

I crunch on apples,
finding starlight trapped inside.

I am the last unicorn.

Watching time run by;
I start to thank my luck.

Acknowledgements

The author would like to thank the editors of the following books where some of these poems previously appeared:

'Wings' from *Another First Poetry Book*, ed. John Foster, copyright © Pie Corbett 1997, OUP; Early drafts and notes for 'Go into –', 'The Things Around You', 'A Brick Is Not a Beautiful Thing', 'A Necklace Poem by Numbers' and 'The Dragon Whistler', copyright © Pie Corbett 2008, appeared in *Jumpstart! Poetry* by Pie Corbett, 2008, Routledge; Early versions of 'Spain – Summer Diary 2001' and 'Remembering' appeared in *How to Teach Poetry Writing at Key Stage 3* by Pie Corbett, copyright © Pie Corbett 2002, David Fulton; 'City Jungle' and 'Biking Free' from *Toughie Toffee*, ed. David Orme, copyright © Pie Corbett 1989, Lions; 'The Tale of the Giant with No Heart' was recorded with Tony Norman, copyright © Pie Corbett 2005.

The following poems were previously published by Macmillan Children's Books:

'Praise poem', 'Early morning, Bradford', 'Poem for Poppy', 'The Day's Eye', 'Galilee', 'The Homecoming – for Emaia' and 'Stars' from *The Works 6*, copyright © Pie Corbett 2007; 'A Poem to Be Spoken Silently . . .' and 'Sunday Morning Diary Poem' from *Ramshackle Rainbow*, copyright © Pie Corbett 2001; 'Are You Sleepwalking?' from *Wild*, ed. James Carter and Graham Denton, copyright © Pie Corbett 2009; 'Early Winter Diary Poem' and 'Take Note' from *The Works: Key Stage 2*, copyright © Pie Corbett 2006; 'My Brother's Pig', 'Owl', 'Smelling Rats', 'A Chance in France' and 'The Poetman' from *Rice, Pie and Moses* (John Rice, Pie Corbett and Brian Moses), copyright © Pie Corbett 1995; 'The Secret Poem' from *The Works 3*, copyright © Pie Corbett 2004; 'The Angel' from *The Works 4*, copyright © Pie Corbett 2005; 'The Tale of the Cleverest Son' from *Poems for Year 4*, copyright © Pie Corbett 2002.

Many thanks to Gaby Morgan.